ONE POEM A DAY

A Writer's Daily Journal of
WORDS & INSPIRATION

Castle Point Books
New York

ONE POEM A DAY. Copyright © 2019 by St. Martin's Press.

All rights reserved. Printed in China.

For information, address St. Martin's Press,
175 Fifth Avenue, New York, N.Y. 10010.

www.castlepointbooks.com
www.stmartins.com

The Castle Point Books trademark is owned by Castle Point Publishing, LLC.
Castle Point books are published and distributed by St. Martin's Press, LLC.

Cover design by Katie Jennings Campbell
Interior design by Joanna Williams

ISBN 978-1-250-20238-3 (trade paperback)

Our books may be purchased in bulk for promotional, educational, or business use.
Please contact your local bookseller or the Macmillan Corporate and Premium Sales Department
at 1-800-221-7945, extension 5442, or by email at MacmillanSpecialMarkets@macmillan.com.

First Edition: April 2019

10 9 8 7 6 5 4 3 2

I WRITE, ERASE, REWRITE

I write, erase, rewrite,
Erase again, and then
A poppy blooms

—Hokushi

Make time to write to your heart's content.

Poetry encourages us to drink in our surroundings, observe the small miracles we often miss, and give voice to our deepest thoughts and feelings. What better way to punctuate and add meaning to our days than with a simple act of poetry.

Everyone has poems inside of them waiting to be freed. *One Poem a Day* is the key to unlocking them and allowing them to take shape on the page. Each page of this journal offers encouragement in the form of a thoughtful, daring, offbeat, or personal poetry prompt. Use the prompts as springboards and begin to fill this book with a flood of poetry that showcases your voice and talent.

Whether you're a self-proclaimed poet, a poetry lover, or a creative soul longing for expression, you'll find peace and satisfaction in the artful adventure of *One Poem a Day*.

Write a poem about something that makes you
uncomfortable. Leave no emotional stone unturned.

Write a rhyming poem about the ocean using any or all of the words provided.

tide • hide • inside • sail • prevail

Consider your best quality and choose an animal to symbolize it. Write a poem celebrating this animal within you.

Describe an everyday object in a way that makes it sound compelling, and make it come alive in your poem.

_____

_____

_____

_____

_____

_____

_____

_____

_____

_____

_____

_____

Write a poem where you compare happiness to a flower.

fresh · plume · open · array · silken · glory

Write an ode to an ex-friend or ex-lover.

Write a prose poem describing a dream you once had. Do not admit that it was a dream.

**Add a new stanza to this Yeats poem below.
Use the same rhyming pattern.**

God guard me from those thoughts men think
In the mind alone;
He that sings a lasting song
Thinks in a marrow-bone;

—from "A Prayer for Old Age," by William Butler Yeats

_____

_____

_____

_____

Write a poem that makes a toast.

Rearrange any or all of the words provided to make a new poem.

In the fire of morning she rises
that lonely star of longing
to begin us again.

_____

_____

_____

_____

_____

_____

_____

_____

_____

_____

Write your favorite poem of all time below, then circle all the little things you love about it. Draw hearts, add notes, underline words, and express your feelings for it all over this page.

Write a poem about love where you repeat
the word *hold* in each line.

Write a poem about loss from the point of view of a child. The loss can be anything from a runaway balloon to a death in the family.

Write a limerick (use an AABBA rhyming scheme)
that reminds you not to take yourself too seriously.

There once was a poet from _____

who _____

_____

_____

_____

Write a 6-word poem about your mother.

Find your most recent social media post
(or that of a friend) and turn it into a poem.

_____

_____

_____

_____

_____

_____

_____

_____

_____

_____

_____

_____

Write a haiku (3 lines, 17 syllables) about your biggest mistake.

Write a poem where you confess something.

Write an acrostic poem using the letters of
your first name.

Invent a new kind of poem with a bizarre
rhyming pattern.

_____

_____

_____

_____

_____

_____

_____

_____

_____

_____

_____

_____

Write a poem about an object and shape the poem to look like the object it is describing.

Write a poem using the next thing someone
says to you as the first line.

Write a 6-word poem about your father.

Write a 2-stanza political poem where the stanzas represent two opposing views.

Write a poem about your celebrity crush.

Write a poem about joy using any or all of the words provided.

balloon • miracle • dawn • skip • hover • rise

Write a poem that is one long question.

Write an ode to your favorite food.

Write a poem from the point of view of someone you wish you knew better.

Write a poem that uses all five senses to describe
an object or setting.

Write an alliterative poem about the passage of time. Repeat a letter sound in each line.

_____

_____

_____

_____

_____

_____

_____

_____

_____

_____

_____

Flip through a book or magazine to find an image that interests you. Write a poem that explains or describes that image.

Write a poem about a leap of faith.

Write a poem that uses your favorite song lyric
as inspiration.

Write a poem where you imagine how the world began.

I wandered lonely as a cloud

That floats on high o'er vales and hills,

When all at once I saw a crowd,

A host, of golden daffodils;

Beside the lake, beneath the trees,

Fluttering and dancing in the breeze.

—from "I Wandered Lonely as a Cloud,"
by William Wordsworth

Write a poem that flows rhythmically using iambic pentameter.

Hint: Place emphasis on the second syllable in each pair of syllables. For example, *I wandered lonely as a cloud*.

Write a poem that should be censored.

Write a poem about a cliché. Use any of the options provided here, or come up with your own.

penny for your thoughts • stop to smell the roses
can't see the forest for the trees • two peas in a pod

Write a poem about riding public transportation.

Write a poem that is an outright lie.

Write a poem about hard work.

Write a scary poem that would make Edgar Allan Poe proud.

_____

_____

_____

_____

_____

_____

_____

_____

And the Raven, never flitting, still is sitting, _still_ is sitting
On the pallid bust of Pallas just above my chamber door;
And his eyes have all the seeming of a demon's that is dreaming,
And the lamp-light o'er him streaming throws his shadow on the floor;

—from "The Raven," by Edgar Allan Poe

Do your best to write the worst poem ever.

Use onomatopoeia (sound words) to write a poem about your day. Use any of the words provided, or use your own.

click • crack • woof • slurp • zing • screech

Add your own set of rhyming words to this Shakespearean sonnet. Then write your own sonnet: 14 lines of iambic pentameter ending in a rhyming couplet.

When my love swears that she is made of _____
I do believe her, though I know she lies,
That she might think me some untutor'd _____,
Unlearned in the world's false subtleties.

—from "Sonnet 138," by William Shakespeare (and you!)

_____

_____

_____

_____

_____

_____

_____

_____

_____

Write an alliterative poem about the rain. Use at
least 3 or 4 words that begin with *r*.

Write a poem about promises.

Write a poem about the best day of your life.

Write (the start of) an epic poem glorifying the adventures of your greatest hero.

Speak, Memory—

                    Of the cunning hero,
The wanderer, blown off course time and again
After he plundered Troy's sacred heights.

                              Speak
Of all the cities he saw, the minds he grasped,
The suffering deep in his heart at sea
As he struggled to survive and bring his men home

—from "The Odyssey," by Homer

Write a poem that you might whisper to someone
you adore. Use all lowercase letters.

Write a poem about a lightning storm. Use any or all of the words provided.

sharp • pang • jagged • streak • lighted • flame

Write a poem about advice you once gave.

Write a poem about a gift you received.

Write the last line of a poem you'll finish
another day.

Write the first line of a poem you'll finish another day.

Write a poem about growing up.

_____

_____

_____

_____

_____

_____

_____

_____

_____

_____

_____

_____

_____

MY LIFE HAS BEEN THE POEM I WOULD HAVE WRIT

My life has been the poem

I would have writ

But I could not both live

and utter it.

—Henry David Thoreau

Write a haiku (3 lines, 17 syllables)
about the Earth.

_____

_____

_____

Write a poem that will make your best friend laugh.

Write a poem that makes light of something serious.

Write a poem that makes a big deal out of nothing.

Take the last text you sent on your cell phone and turn it into a poem.

_____

_____

_____

_____

_____

_____

_____

_____

_____

_____

_____

_____

Write a poem about your favorite novel.

Write a poem about yourself from your parent's point of view.

Write a poem set in a fantasy world.

Write a poem about the last thing you searched for online.

Write a poem about a historic moment.

Write a poem that predicts the future.

Write a poem about flying. Use any or all of the words provided.

careen • cascade • lightness • invisible • valiant • wings

_____

_____

_____

_____

_____

_____

_____

_____

_____

_____

_____

_____

Write a poem for an upcoming birthday.

Write a poem that begins and ends with
the same line.

_____

_____

_____

_____

_____

_____

_____

_____

_____

_____

_____

_____

Write a poem about something broken.

Write a sensual poem about your first or most recent love.

Twilight—and you
Quiet—the stars;
Snare of the shine of your teeth,
Your provocative laughter,
The gloom of your hair;
Lure of you, eye and lip;
Yearning, yearning,
Languor, surrender;

—from "El Beso," by Angelina Weld Grimké

Write a poem using at least one word from
a foreign language.

Write a poem about your age. Use the number in the title or in the poem.

Write a poem that explains why you like poetry.

Write a poem about a river. Use any or all of the words provided.

cascade • trickle • stones • tension • flow • wander

Write a poem that makes you hungry.

Write a poem about your ancestors.

Write a poem that uses at least two similes.

_____

_____

_____

_____

_____

_____

_____

_____

_____

_____

_____

_____

Write a poem that's formatted like a letter.

Write a bedtime lullaby for a child or an adult.

Write a poem in the form of a to-do list.

Write a poem about a relationship you're building.

_____

_____

_____

_____

_____

_____

_____

_____

_____

Before I built a wall I'd ask to know
What I was walling in or walling out,
And to whom I was like to give offence.
Something there is that doesn't love a wall,

—from "Mending Wall," by Robert Frost

Write a poem about a weary traveler.

Write a poem about war.

Write a poem about the nature of men.

Write a poem about the nature of women.

Write a poem about money.

Write a poem about the moon.

The Moon was but a Chin of Gold
A Night or two ago—
And now she turns Her perfect Face
Upon the World below—

—from "The Moon was but a Chin of Gold," by Emily Dickinson

Write a poem that personifies an object.

Write a poem in the form of a spreadsheet.

Write a poem that compares night and day.

Write a hate poem that transforms into
a love poem.

Write a poem about your favorite holiday.

Make like Shakespeare and compare someone to a summer's day.

_____

_____

_____

_____

_____

_____

_____

_____

Shall I compare thee to a summer's day?
Thou art more lovely and more temperate:
Rough winds do shake the darling buds of May,
And summer's lease hath all too short a date;

—from "Sonnet 18," by William Shakespeare

Write a poem about a red wheelbarrow and
dedicate it to William Carlos Williams.

Write a poem about a whale.

Write a poem about your body.

Write a poem to your younger self.

Write a poem about outer space.

Write a poem about the life of an insect.

Write a poem using your favorite word of all time.

Write a poem with a very formal tone.

Write a poem about a party.

Write a 5-line poem that sums up your day.

Write a poem about a legendary monster.

Write a poem about winter. Use any or all of the words provided.

stark • air • encased • flake • sheet • warmth

Write a poem about an overdue library book.

Write a poem that is a list of your favorite things.

Write a tender poem about something or someone you hate.

Write a poem about patience. Leave lots of extra space between lines.

Write a poem about madness with lots of dashes
    and surprising—
            or jarring—
line breaks.

Write a tiny poem about a tiny object.

Write a poem that forgets where it started.

Write a poem about choices. Give it two different endings.

_____

_____

_____

_____

_____

_____

_____

_____

_____

_____

_____

_____

_____

Write a patriotic poem.

Write a poem about pain or suffering that you
have endured.

Write a poem about the last book you read.

Write a narrative poem about what magic means to you.

Write a poem about where you grew up.

Write a poem about a garden.

Write a limerick about your commute.

There once was a _____

who _____

_____

_____

_____

Write a poem that begins with a dictionary entry.

Write a poem about a sport.

Write an ode to an antiquated device.

Write an epic poem starring you as the hero.

Write a poem that compares anger to fire.

_____

_____

_____

_____

_____

_____

_____

_____

_____

_____

_____

_____

Write a poem about guilt. Use any or all of the words provided.

hidden • weighty • stone • emerge • shadow • loom

Write a poem about a god or goddess.

Write a poem about autumn leaves.

Write a poem about a seashell using the words
provided in any order.

iridescent • shield • lying • undiscovered

Write a poem entitled "Two Truths and a Lie."

Write a poem about a musical instrument.

Write a haiku (3 lines, 17 syllables)
about the setting sun.

_____

_____

_____

Write a poem about a painting that inspires you.

Write a poem about a morning ritual.

Write a stream-of-consciousness poem.

Write a prose poem about the last time you were
(or felt) drunk.

_____

_____

_____

_____

_____

_____

_____

_____

_____

It will lap and scratch
As I swallow it down;
And I shall feel it as a serpent of fire,
Coiling and twisting in my belly.

—from "Vintage," by Amy Lowell

Write a poem that uses a locked door as a symbol.

Write a poem about something dangerous you did.

Write a poem that recounts the events of your favorite story.

Write a limerick about someone who
drives you crazy.

There once was a _____

who_____

_____

_____

_____

Write a poem about hope.

Write a LOUD poem that is all caps
and exclamations.

Write a poem that apologizes for something.

Write a poem that forgives someone.

Rewrite this timeless verse, but replace as many words as you can with synonyms.

Twinkle, twinkle, little star,
How I wonder what you are!
Up above the world so high,
Like a diamond in the sky.

—from "The Star," by Jane Taylor

_____

_____

_____

_____

_____

_____

_____

_____

_____

_____

Write a poem about small talk.

Write a poem that uses your address in one of the lines.

Write a darker or more modern rendition of this classic children's rhyme.

Row, row, row your boat,
Gently down the stream,
Merrily, merrily, merrily, merrily,
Life is but a dream.

—Anonymous

_____

_____

_____

_____

_____

_____

_____

_____

_____

Write a poem entitled "The Meaning of Life,"
and make it about anything you want.

Write a poem about a reunion.

Write a poem to your virtual home assistant:
the one that hears everything you say.

Write a poem that reveals your true identity.

Write a poem about a bird. Use any or all of the words provided.

trill • thoughts • perched • heights • endless

Write a poem that's also a personal ad for
a dating site.

Write a poem using only words that start with
a, *t*, or *w*. Use any or all of the words provided.

all • we • took • was • wasted • time • and

Write an elegy for someone you love.

Fill in the blanks below to create a poem.

Across the great _____,

my _____

Along the open _____,

my mind _____

Above the grand _____

my heart _____

Who says we cannot _____.

Write a poem that compares fate to a carousel.
Use any or all of the words provided.

ride • steed • carried • bound • cease • choose

Write a poem about marriage.

Write a poem about the road you didn't choose.

Write a poem about beginnings.

Change this poem into a 17-syllable haiku.

Hearing thunder
a tremble of regret
shakes my heart.

_____

_____

_____

Write a poem about karma.

Write a poem about grief.

Write a poem about parenthood.

Finish this fill-in-the-blank poem.

Her hair streams _____ behind her

as she rides to _____

Who knows when she will _____

One never _____ days like these

Write an unfinished poem and ask a friend
to finish it.

Complete the poem by adding a rhyming couplet after each line.

The earth is cool beneath my toes

_____

The birds all sing a merry tune

_____

I find my lover in the grove

_____

We lingered there all summer long

_____

Write a poetic response to Walt Whitman's question in the poem "Miracles."

To me the sea is a continual miracle,
The fishes that swim—the rocks—the motion of the waves—the
    ships with men in them,
What stranger miracles are there?

Write a poem about this particular day of the week
and what it means to you.

Write a poem that gives a voice to someone whose voice has been stifled.

Write a poem about a snake.

Write a poem that works like a conversation.

Write a poem about someone else's pain.

Write a poem about a place of worship.

Write a poem about a constellation.

Write a poem for your sibling (or the one you wish you had).

Write a limerick that's dead serious.

There once was a _____

who _____

_____

_____

_____

Rewrite one of your poems from a previous page and break the lines in new and surprising ways. Read both poems out loud and decide which one you like better.

Write a poem about a time when you found
inner strength. Use any or all of the words provided.

rage • fire • unfurl • clamorous • soul

No coward soul is mine,
No trembler in the world's storm-troubled sphere:
I see Heaven's glories shine,
And faith shines equal, arming me from fear.

—from "No Coward Soul is Mine," by Emily Brontë

Rearrange any or all of the words provided to make a new poem.

today we believe that
tomorrow will knock and
lead us to an open door

_____

_____

_____

_____

_____

_____

_____

_____

_____

Write a poem about littering.

Write a poem that wants to be sung.

Write a poem in a secret code.

Write a 15-word poem about the first time
you did something.

Choose a poem from an earlier page and write it backward (from last word to first word). Edit as needed and make it a whole new poem.

Write a poem about being in love, even if you've never been in love.

Write a poem about being in jail, even if you've never been in jail.

Write a poem about failure.

Write a narrative poem that makes you
want to cry.

Write a haiku (3 lines, 17 syllables)
about junk mail.

_____

_____

_____

Write a poem about disappearing.
End it abruptly.

Write a poem about one of your favorite photographs.

Write a poem about someone digging a hole.

Write a poem where bees are a metaphor for dangerous thoughts.

Write a poem you'd be embarrassed to show
your parents.

Write a poem about your feet.

Write a poem about a tree using any or all of the words provided.

canopy • ogre • shade • steady • rooted • held

Write a poem about the last fight you had.

Write a poem about an amazing smile.

Write a poem where you compare fear to a tiger.
Use any or all of the words provided.

gnash · claw · chase · track · mercy · terror

Write a poem about skinny-dipping.

Write a poem that references a line from your
favorite book.

Write a poem about a lighthouse.

Write a poem about looking down from
a great height.

Write a poem about a mall Santa.

Write a poem about a scent that elicits
strong memories.

Write a poem where each line begins with the
same letter.

Write a poem about a moustache.

Write a poem about a petty crime.

Write a poem about the *Titanic*. Use any or all of the words provided.

hulking • voyage • sequined • revelers • cargo • stories

Write a poem that brags about what a good
poem it is.

My soul is awakened, my spirit is soaring
And carried aloft on the wings of the breeze;
For above and around me the wild wind is roaring,
Arousing to rapture the earth and the seas.

—from "Lines Composed in a Wood on a Windy Day," by Anne Brontë

Write a 9-word poem about today's weather.

Use a front-page headline as **the title of** today's poem.

Write a poem that takes the form
of a yearbook write-up.

place photo here

Write a poem about a favorite television show.

Write a poem about a grandparent.

Write a poem about a building that's meaningful to you.

Write a poem about bad drivers.

Write a poem where each line starts with
the word *once*.

Write a funny poem called "How to Write Poetry."

Write a poem about a famous speech. Use some of the words from the speech in your poem.

Write a limerick about a turning point in your life.

There once was a _____

who _____

_____

_____

_____

Write a poem about a ghost. When you're finished, erase half of the words.

Write a poetic response to Robert Frost's poem "Fire and Ice."

FIRE AND ICE

Some say the world will end in fire,
Some say in ice.
From what I've tasted of desire
I hold with those who favor fire.
But if it had to perish twice,
I think I know enough of hate
To know that for destruction ice
Is also great,
And would suffice.

_____

_____

_____

_____

_____

_____

_____

Write a nonsense poem that would make
Lewis Carroll proud. Include at least one
fantastical creature.

Write a transcendental poem that worships nature.

Write a poem about innocence.

Write a poem that begins with this line:
The silence finds its way to me.

Write a poem about cleaning.

Write a poem that is a time capsule from the year you were born.

Write a quatrain (a 4-line poem) that ends
in the rhyming words provided:

_____ land

_____ grow

_____ sleep

_____ know.

I am not yours, not lost in you,
Not lost, although I long to be
Lost as a candle lit at noon,
Lost as a snowflake in the sea.

—from "I Am Not Yours," by Sara Teasdale

Write a poem that ends in this line:
And never have I loved you more.

_____

_____

_____

_____

_____

_____

_____

_____

_____

_____

_____

_____

_____

_____

Write a narrative poem with an unreliable narrator.

_____

_____

_____

_____

_____

_____

_____

_____

_____

_____

_____

_____

Write a poem about graffiti.

Write a 10-word poem about pride. Use any or all of the words provided.

mirror • blind • vision • distorted • glory

Use any or all of the words provided to make
a new poem.

open • hand • lantern • glow • memories

_____

_____

_____

_____

_____

_____

_____

_____

_____

_____

_____

_____

Write a poem about an empty dinner table.

Write a poem about a rainbow.

Write a poem about a deep, dark forest.

Write a poem that repeats the word *remain*
at least 4 times.

Write a poem about a clown.

Write an acrostic poem from the word *home.*
Each line must begin with the letter provided.

H _____

O _____

M _____

E _____ .

Write a poem about cruelty.

Write a poem about a runaway horse.

Write a poem that has a moral lesson.

_____

_____

_____

_____

_____

_____

_____

_____

_____

_____

_____

_____

Write a poem that compares your heart to a bird
or other animal.

My heart is like a singing bird
    Whose nest is in a watered shoot;
My heart is like an apple tree
    Whose boughs are bent with thickset fruit;
My heart is like a rainbow shell
    That paddles in a halcyon sea;
My heart is gladder than all these
    Because my love is come to me.

—from "A Birthday," by Christina Rossetti

Write a poem that celebrates your state or region.

Write a poem that pays tribute to writers everywhere.

Write a poem about moving on. Use any or all
of the words provided.

past • slung • luggage • strength • forge

Write a poem about fast food.

Write a poem (dedicated to Rudyard Kipling)
where every other line starts with *If.*

If you can talk with crowds and keep your virtue,
    Or walk with Kings—nor lose the common touch,
If neither foes nor loving friends can hurt you,
    If all men count with you, but none too much;
If you can fill the unforgiving minute
    With sixty seconds' worth of distance run,
Yours is the Earth and everything that's in it,
    And—which is more—you'll be a Man, my son!

—from "If," by Rudyard Kipling

Write a poem about this decade.

Write a poem about a foreign country.

Write a poem about dancing.

Write a haiku (3 lines, 17 syllables) about morning.

_____

_____

_____

Write a poem about a glorious vision.

_____

_____

_____

_____

_____

_____

_____

_____

_____

_____

_____

THE SEA OF GLASS

I looked and saw a sea

                roofed over with rainbows,

In the midst of each

                two lovers met and departed;

Then the sky was full of faces

                with gold glories behind them.

—Ezra Pound

Write a poem that's also a fairy tale.

Write a poem that describes the view out of the closest window.

_____

_____

_____

_____

_____

_____

_____

_____

_____

_____

_____

_____

Write a poem using a knock-knock joke format.

Knock, knock.

Who's there?

_____

_____ who?

_____

_____

Write a poem about a computer error message.

Write a poem about an item in your pocket.

Write a poem that quotes a verse from one of your
favorite poems.

Write a poem about someone else's secret.

Write a poem about a lottery winner.

Write a poem that compares jealousy to a dragon.

Write a poem about sleeping. Use the letter z
as many times as possible.

Write a poem about a mountain. Use any or all
of the words provided.

crest • climb • skyward • gossamer • cloudscape

Write a poem that ends in this line:
the scribbled relics of my mind.

Write an optimistic poem about your future.

Find a poem that inspires you to write more
poetry. Copy it here.

Write a poem about a kiss.